DINOSAURS
COLORING BOOK

Anna Pomaska

DOVER PUBLICATIONS
Garden City, New York

Bibliographical Note

BOOST Dinosaurs Coloring Book, first published by Dover Publications in
2013, is a revised edition of *Dinosaurs,* originally published by Dover in 1998.

International Standard Book Number
ISBN-13: 978-0-486-49415-9
ISBN-10: 0-486-49415-2

Manufactured in the United States by LSC Communications Book LLC
49415206   2021
www.doverpublications.com

TYRANNOSAURUS (tie-RAN-oh-SAW-rus)

This was one of the biggest meat-eating dinosaurs. It had very big, sharp teeth.

 RI.1.7 Use the illustrations and details in a text to describe its key ideas. Also **RI.1.1, RF.1.3.c, L.1.6; RI.2.1, RF.2.3.b, L.2.6.**

TRICERATOPS (try-SER-a-tops)

Count the horns on this dinosaur. You will understand why its name means "three-horned face."

Here is a Triceratops mother and baby. When grown up, these dinosaurs were as big as elephants. They liked to travel in large herds.

The hungry Tyrannosaurus wants to make a meal of the plant-eating Triceratops.

CCSS RI.1.7 Use the illustrations and details in a text to describe its key ideas. Also **RI.1.3, RI.1.10, RF.1.3.c, L.1.6; RI.2.7, RI.2.10, RF.2.3.b, L.2.6.**

Triceratops does not like to fight. But it can protect itself with its three sharp horns.

 RI.1.6 Distinguish between information provided by pictures or other illustrations and information provided by the words in a text. Also **RI.1.7, RF.1.3, SL.1.1.c, SL.1.4; RI.2.6, RI.2.7, RF.2.3, SL.2.1.c.**

ELASMOSAURUS (ee-LAZ-moe-SAW-rus)

Elasmosaurus was a giant sea reptile. It had a very long neck.
It used its neck to catch fish.

  RI.1.4 Ask and answer questions to help determine or clarify the meaning of words and phrases in a text. Also **RI.1.6, RF.1.3.a, RF.1.3.g; RI.2.4, RI.2.6, RF.2.3.c.**

STEGOSAURUS (STEG-oh-SAW-rus)

This dinosaur had large bony plates. The plates stuck up out of its back. It also had four long spikes on the end of its tail to protect itself.

 RI.1.7 Use the illustrations and details in a text to describe its key ideas. Also **RI.1.4, RF.1.3.a, RF.1.4, SL.1.2, SL.1.4; RI.2.4, RI.2.7, RF.2.4, SL.2.2.**

CAMARASAURUS (kam-AR-a-SAW-rus)

Camarasaurus was a gentle giant. It was big, heavy, and slow moving.
It ate only plants.

ARCHAEOPTERYX (ark-ee-OP-ter-ix)

Archaeopteryx looked like a little dinosaur with wings.
It had feathers and is the first known bird.

ANKYLOSAURUS (an-KY-low-SAW-rus)

This dinosaur ate only plants. It had an armor of bone and horns and a tail club that it used to protect itself.

 RI.1.1 Ask and answer questions about key details in a text. Also **RI.1.7, RF.1.4.a, L.1.4.a; RI.2.1, RI.2.7, RF.2.4.a, L.2.4.a.**

DEINONYCHUS (DIE-no-NIKE-us)

The name of this dinosaur means "terrible claw."
It had a big claw shaped like a curved sword on each foot.

RI.1.4 Ask and answer questions to help determine or clarify the meaning of words and phrases in a text. Also **RI.1.7, RF.1.3.g, SL.1.2, SL.1.4, L.1.6; RI.2.4, RI.2.7, RF.2.3.f, SL.2.2, L.2.6.**

APATOSAURUS (a-PAT-oh-SAW-rus)

This dinosaur was once called Brontosaurus. Its bones were discovered by two different scientists. They thought they had discovered two different dinosaurs.

 RI.1.3 Describe the connection between two individuals, events, ideas, or pieces of information in a text. Also **RI.1.1, RF.1.4, SL.1.2; RI.2.1, RI.2.3, RF.2.3.d, RF.2.4, SL.2.2.**

Apatosaurus was a very heavy and tall dinosaur.
It ate only plants, but lots and lots of them!

 RI.1.1 Ask and answer questions about key details in a text. Also **RI.1.7, RF.1.3.e, SL.1.1;**
RI.2.1, RI.2.7, RF.2.3.a, SL.2.1.

ICHTHYOSAURUS (ICK-thee-oh-SAW-rus)

Ichthyosaurus was an ocean reptile. It had fins and flippers.
It looked and swam like dolphins of today.

 RI.1.2 Identify the main topic and retell key details of a text. Also **RI.1.3, RI.1.6, RF.1.3.g, L.1.6; RI.2.3, RI.2.6, RF.2.3.f, L.2.6.**

PSITTACOSAURUS (si-TAK-oh-SAW-rus)

Psittacosaurus had a beak which made this dinosaur look like a parrot.

 RI.1.7 Use the illustrations and details in a text to describe its key ideas. Also **RI.1.1, RI.1.6, RF.1.3.b, SL.1.2, SL.1.4; RI.2.1, RI.2.6, RI.2.7, RF.2.3.f, SL.2.2.**

PARASAUROLOPHUS (par-a-SAWR-oh-LOAF-us)

This was a duck-billed dinosaur. It made loud sounds through the tube on its head.

 RI.1.6 Distinguish between information provided by pictures or other illustrations and information provided by the words in a text. Also **RI.1.7, RF.1.3.f, SL.1.2; RI.2.6, RI.2.7, RF.2.3.b, SL.2.2.**

CORYTHOSAURUS (ko-RITH-oh-SAW-rus)

This was another duck-billed dinosaur.
It made a loud noise through a fan-shaped crest on its head.

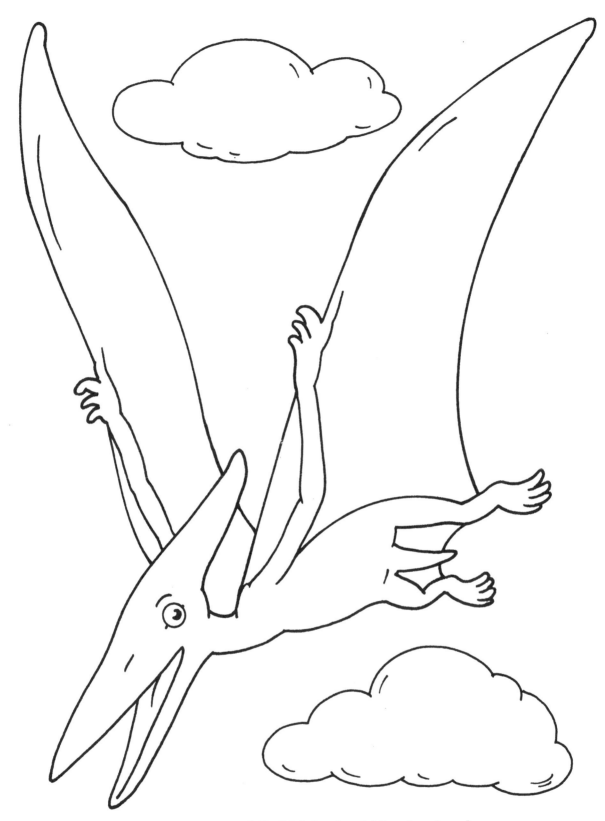

PTERANODON (tair-AN-oh-don)

Pteranodon was a reptile with very long wings.
It could glide on the air and swoop down to catch a fish from the sea.

CCSS **RI.1.6** Distinguish between information provided by pictures or other illustrations and information provided by the words in a text. Also **RI.1.1, RI.1.7, RF.1.3, SL.1.4, L.1.4.a; RI.2.1, RI.2.6, RI.2.7, RF.2.3, L.2.4.a.**

IGUANODON (i-GWA-no-DON)

Iguanodon had a big spike for a thumb that helped protect it.

 RI.1.7 Use the illustrations and details in a text to describe its key ideas. Also **RI.1.1,**
RI.1.10, RF.1.3.c, L.1.5.c; RI.2.1, RI.2.7, RI.2.10, L.2.5.a.

OVIRAPTOR (OVE-ih-RAP-tor)

Experts think that Oviraptor sat on its eggs. This kept them safe and warm.

 RI.1.3 Describe the connection between two individuals, events, ideas, or pieces of information in a text. Also **RI.1.6, SL.1.2, SL.1.4; RI.2.3, RI.2.6, SL.2.2.**

SPINOSAURUS (SPINE-o-SAW-rus)

This strange dinosaur had a huge sail along its back.

BAROSAURUS (BAR-oh-SAW-rus)

Barosaurus was a giant dinosaur. It had a very long neck and tail.
It could reach leaves at the top of tall trees.

A baby Barosaurus stayed close to its mother for protection until it grew up.
By then, it weighed more than 8 elephants!

 RI.1.3 Describe the connection between two individuals, events, ideas, or pieces of information in a text. Also **RI.1.1, RI.1.7, SL.1.1.c, SL.1.4; RI.2.1, RI.2.3, RI.2.7, SL.2.1.c.**

PROTOCERATOPS (pro-toe-SER-a-tops)

Protoceratops laid many eggs in nests made of sand.
Its babies hatched by cracking open the shells and climbing out.

STRUTHIOMIMUS (STROOTH-ee-oh-MIME-us)

Struthiomimus means "ostrich mimic."
This dinosaur acted and looked like a big bird without feathers.

 RI.1.4 Ask and answer questions to help determine or clarify the meaning of words and phrases in a text. Also **RI.1.7, RI.1.10, RF.1.1, SL.1.2, SL.1.4; RI.2.4, RI.2.7, RI.2.10, SL.2.2.**

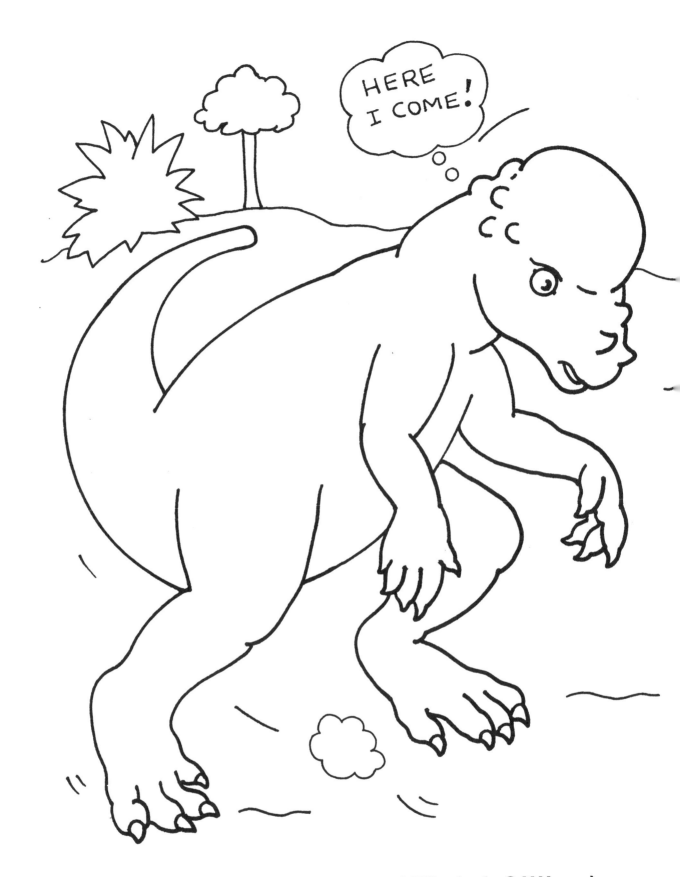

PACHYCEPHALOSAURUS (PAK-ee-CEF-al-oh-SAW-rus)

These dinosaurs had hard bony heads that looked like crash helmets.

 RI.1.6 Distinguish between information provided by pictures or other illustrations and information provided by the words in a text. Also **RI.1.4, RI.1.7, RF.1.4.a, SL.1.1.c; RI.2.4, RI.2.6, RI.2.7, RF.2.4.a, SL.2.1.c.**

They used their heads in butting contests to see who was stronger.
The two in this picture are about to bump into each other!

 RI.1.7 Use the illustrations and details in a text to describe its key ideas. Also **RI.1.6,**
RF.1.4.a, L.1.4.a, L.1.6; RI.2.6, RI.2.7, RF.2.4.a, L.2.4.a, L.2.6.

STYRACOSAURUS (sty-RAK-oh-SAW-rus)

Styracosaurus looked very scary with its horns and spikes.
It liked to eat only plants.

 RI.1.6 Distinguish between information provided by pictures or other illustrations and information provided by the words in a text. Also **RI.1.7, RI.1.10, RF.1.3.f, SL.1.4; RI.2.6, RI.2.7, RI.2.10, RF.2.3.d.**

LAMBEOSAURUS (LAM-bee-oh-SAW-rus)

Lambeosaurus has come down to the river for a drink of water.
Like Styracosaurus, it ate only plants.

 RI.1.1 Ask and answer questions about key details in a text. Also RI.1.7, RF.1.3, SL.1.1; RI.2.1, RI.2.7, RF.2.3, SL.2.1.

MAIASAURA (MY-a-SAW-ra)

Maiasaura was a good mother. It stayed with its children and brought them leaves to eat until they grew old enough to care of themselves.

 RI.1.6 Distinguish between information provided by pictures or other illustrations and information provided by the words in a text. Also **RI.1.1, RF.1.3.a, L.1.6; RI.2.1, RI.2.6, RF.2.3.b, L.2.6.**